Front cover illustration: Village Road, Nannerch

Back cover illustration: Tai Cochion Cottages

© Copyright 2018 Brian Bennett

All rights reserved

No part of this publication to be reproduced, stored in a retrieval system or transmitted in any form or by any means, electronic, mechanical, photocopying, recording or otherwise, without the prior permission of the Copyright holder.

i

INTRODUCTION / FOREWORD

In compiling this small publication on the village of Nannerch, it is a collection of personal memories of incidents, illustrations, occurrences, etc., which have taken place in the Community over the last century or so. This book is not and never intended as a historical reference book, but noticing that only a couple of small publications have ever been written or published on the subject to my knowledge, since the first reference of the village name in 1254. I am of the impression that another publication is warranted and surely well overdue.

So what gives me the right to publish a book on the subject ? Well, first and foremost, I was born and bred in the Parish, confirmed in the local Church, attended the local village primary school, albeit for only two years. I was employed in my school days delivering bread and groceries for J Davies & Sons (Nannerch Mill Bakery) and still having family members in the village, hopefully gives me some form of license to print this publication.

My grandfather Edward Evan Watkin came to the area in 1926 as a tenant farmer on the Penbedw Estate, farming Plas Yw, one of the most ancient establishments in the Community, if not in the County, before leaving to farm Tyddyn Onn for six years before finally moving again to Bryn Charlotte, which is on the eastern edge of the Parish near to Cilcain Hall - all these farms being incorporated in the Penbedw Estate at the time. I myself and my twin brother David were born and raised at Bryn Charlotte soon after the end of the Second World War, from where we both started at Nannerch VP School in September 1951, often walking the two mile distance to and from school.

continued...

Good old days remembered with relish and being taught by Miss Alwen James, a firm but fair Headmistress, still highly respected by older pupils / villagers decades after her retirement. I am a great believer that these illustrations / memories, etc., are catalogued and recorded before they get lost and forgotten about in the mist of time. One thing that has become abundantly clear in compiling this book is not what is included, but what is excluded ! Such is the abundance of historical interest that Nannerch village and Parish possesses that it is impossible to include everything in one small publication. My biggest regret in publishing this book is that I did not do it years earlier.

This is my first attempt at any form of publication and I can only hope that any readers, young or old, find it of interest and enjoy reading / browsing through this illustrated book, as much as I have enjoyed compiling it ! Happy reading !

BRIAN BENNETT

April 2018

NANNERCH

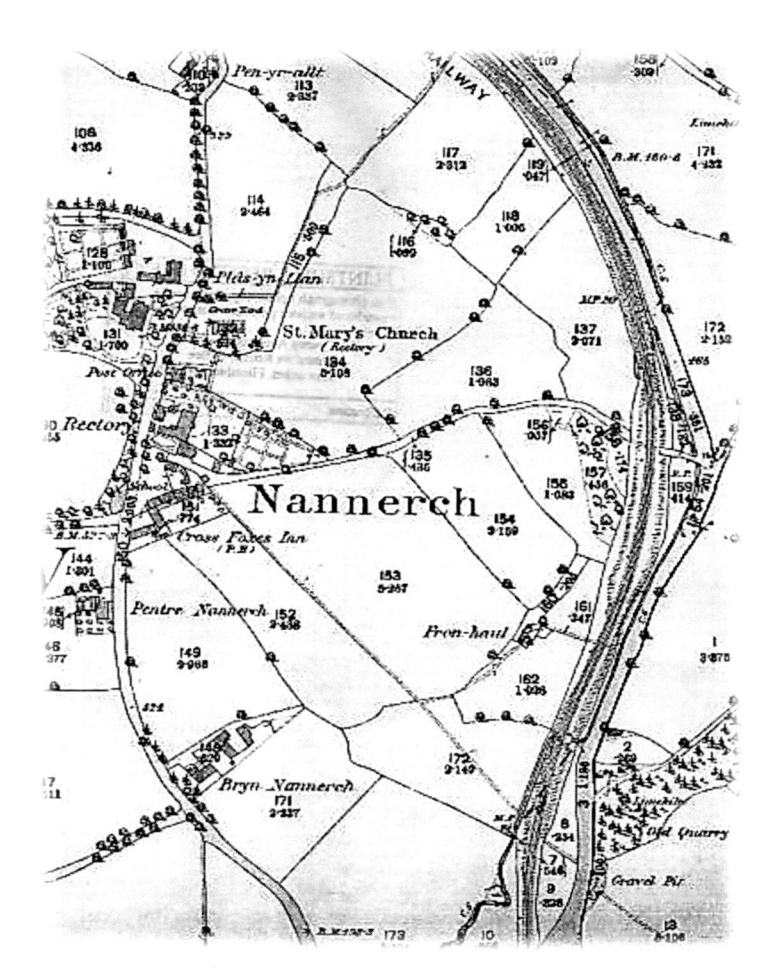

c1871

iv

VICTORIAN NANNERCH

This early map of Nannerch Village depicting just how sparsely populated the village centre was in Victorian times. This being the case until predominantly the second half of the twentieth century, before the construction of the modern housing developments as we know it today. Notice the railway is boldly illustrated on the right hand side of the image, having been opened in 1869 just prior to the alleged date of this print. The present school is not shown on the map, whilst the school of the day is shown by the Cross Foxes Inn, having not been constructed until 1894. The siting of the Post Office is of interest ! It appears to be on village road, but near the Church, somewhere near or where Y Hen Bwthyn is situated today. Another misnomer is the title of the Church, being referred to as St Mary's, but when it was built and consecrated in 1852-53 it was renamed St Michael & All Angels. The village pond on the corner of Pen y felin Road is also evident. The village centre of the day, would only consist of no more than a dozen residences but the Parish was still able to support among other businesses a Post Office / General Shop, School, three Chapels, Church and Rectory, Bakery, several corn mills, Smithy, two Public Houses, and a newly opened railway station. A truly fascinating insight / image of how the village and surrounding area appeared in the mid to late Victorian period.

A typical rural village that was self sufficient and met its own needs - this before the age of supermarkets, the revolution in communications, and the growth of internet trading. A true insight into what we have lost and what we have gained as a rural community over the last century or so.

NANNERCH TODAY

This modern day aerial photograph of the village centre showing the recent housing developments, especially on the southerly part (left) illustrating how much increase in housing that has taken place over the last half century or so. This is borne out of the fact that the population of the Parish has fluctuated between 347 in the 1921 census, falling to 247 in 1971, but increasing to 496 in the 2011 poll. Nowadays, the vast majority of the working population either commute to work by private transport or generally work from home. Traditional sources of employment, for example, in Nannerch's case, agriculture, mining, to name just two examples, these together with other small cottage industries have long since disappeared.

The road network of the village has changed little over the centuries, still following the same routes that early inhabitants, drovers and travellers used, and followed since the formation of the settlement, in all probability over a thousand years ago.

Nannerch is no different from thousands of similar villages across the country and has had to adapt to the changes of the 21st century. Looking at the past photographic images printed in this book, I find it very sad, but inevitable, surveying the changes that have taken place over the last century or so. Thankfully, the village has retained its identity and individuality in many cases which present day Nannerch folk should be justifiably proud of.

Nannerch Village

Village Road c1910

A tranquil view of Village Road taken around the early part of the 20th century with Pentref very prominent in the centre.   The General Stores and Post Office is just to the left of the horses & carts displaying early advertising signage on the facing wall.   The Town Hall can just be seen near left, but no phone box is evident in those days. The War Memorial site was from all accounts just a village pond before the construction of the memorial stone in the 1930s.

Village Road c1930

The second of four similar views taken from the same spot, depicting what changes have occurred in the village centre over the c110 year time difference. This particular image, judging by the automobile, was taken c1930. A point of interest is the telegraph pole seen in front of the vehicle, but the telephone kiosk is absent. This telegraph pole and lineage was to enable telegrams to be sent and delivered to the nearby Post Office before the telephone had reached the village.

Village Road c1960

An interesting c1960 view looking south down Village Road, which was taken by Mr R F Higgen formally of Fron Haul, Nannerch, with his Ford Popular car being the only vehicle evident. This image would be taken just prior to the building of the new housing development which today skirt Village Road and Pen y felin Road, and approximately two decades before the cottages on the Smithy yard near left were constructed.

Village Road, Nannerch.

A present day view from the same spot.   Interesting to note the changes that have occurred over the last hundred years or more between the four images.   The appearance of the telephone box and the war memorial are two obvious additions.   Pentref (centre) still stands but now hidden by trees, dating back to 1804.   It is difficult to imagine that the old World War I tank stood on the facing corner for almost 20 years in the decades between the two World Wars.   The now disused red phone box is today a listed building in the care of the Community Council.

Village View c1930

A rare picture postcard image taken from where the Bryn Dedwydd modern bungalow development is situated today showing the side elevation of the unmistakable Tai Cochion cottages. Since this image was taken the old Police Station now named Bendegedig, this with two modern residences, together with the pensioners bungalows have appeared. The Cross Foxes Inn is prominent (centre) with the Church spire visible far right.

Tai Cochion

Tai Cochion cottages - built for the Buddicoms of Penbedw Estate in the late 1870s being designed by the noted Chester Architect namely, John Douglas. Number 1 was for decades used as the village Police Station. This being the case until c1950 when the new Police Station nearby was erected. The cottages are Grade II listed buildings and are described as properties of the vernacular revival style with tiled hipped rooves.

Memorial, Nannerch.

War Memorial c1930s

Another picture post card showing the War Memorial and Village Road, taken shortly after it's erection in c1930.   The monument itself does not bear any names of the fallen from either WW1 or WW2, but a memorial plaque inside the Church commemorates the fact that 65 young men / women from the Parish were called into action in WW1 conflict alone.   Sadly, two perished in action and at least two more died from a flu related illness.   This figure would be a significantly high percentage of the Parish population of the day and it is impossible to gauge the impact of such a traumatic time must have had on the village family and social life of the period.

Nannerch Village 1914 - 1918

Like thousands of similar villages across the country Nannerch was no different, ie. sending young men and women to the battle front, and helping provide the nation with the necessary agricultural and food needs required.   Some of the displayed images in this book are taken from the 1914-1918 WW1 period which typified the rural environment that the village enjoyed.   One interesting point about the village, albeit a couple of years after the war ended, was the arrival of a WW1 armoured tank which had been involved in the war effort in France and was brought to Nannerch by Major Buddicom of Penbedw Hall who had played a major role in its design and development.   It is believed it was brought as a memorial to his only son Lt. Walter Digby Buddicom who was sadly killed in action during the conflict.   The tank came to Nannerch in c1919 arriving by rail at Rhydymwyn Railway Station and journeying the three mile distance by road to Nannerch.   The reason being that the authorities of the day decreed that the road bridges at Hendre were not strong enough to support the weight of the armoured vehicle.   As the tank made the journey by road from Rhydymwyn, it was met on the way by the village school children excited by its imminent arrival.   The girls were allowed to ride on the vehicle whilst the boys walked behind.   Not many Health & Safety issues in those days !   The tank stood on the corner of Village Road and Pen y felin Road for many years becoming a symbol of the WW1 effort and also a tourist attraction for the neighbourhood and, not forgetting, it being a plaything for a generation of Nannerch school children.   When the dark clouds of war once more appeared on the horizon the tank was dismantled and despatched to help with the forthcoming war effort of WW2.

Village Road, Nannerch c1930s

The pride of my collection for two reasons. Firstly, to the best of my knowledge this is the only photographic image that exists of the first WW1 tank in situ on the corner of Pen y felin Road. Secondly, a view of the policeman of the day (Mr Stephen Jones) with his bicycle outside the Police Station of the day which pre war was situated at No.1 Tai Cochion. A truly iconic view of Nannerch in the pre war era.

Village Road

A present day view of Tai Cochion cottages taken from the same spot, with the distinctive brickwork very evident. Again, approximately ninety years between the two images and it is always of interest to note how much or, indeed, how little this village scene has changed over the years. The two most notable differences being the removal of the old WW1 tank and the absence of a village constable.

WW1 Tank, Schoolchildren & Staff c1920

Children & Teachers names

Children and Staff of the village school pictured standing / sitting proudly on or by the recently arrived WW1 armoured tank.   Very few villages could boast of such a huge memorial structure which was a subject of fascination and intrigue for nearly twenty years between the two wars.

Standing (Left to Right)

George James / George Halsall / John Roberts / Fred Thomas / Les Jones / ? / Charlie Partington / Nellie Pritchard / Magdalene Jones (kneeling) / Celia Williams (kneeling) / May Mackintosh (kneeling) / Maggie Mackintosh / Gladys Williams / Cyril Williams / ? / Enid Davies

Sitting (Left to Right)

Charles Wilcox / Percy Jones / Frank Vernon / Thomas John Jones / Trevor Jones / Idwal Davies / Joe Wood / Emlyn Davies

Bottom

Teacher - Miss Brown (Left) / Teacher - Miss Edwards (Right)

Pupils include Cissy Edwards / Bill Hughes / Glyn Davies / Elsie & Dot Watson / Gwen Cave / Dorothy Jones / Mary Byrne / Sally Hughes / Doris James / Sisters - Dorothy & Elsie Jones

THE POST OFFICE, NANNERCH.

Village Post Office c1900

Another early rare 20th century picture postcard of Village Road looking north with the mode of transport of the day very evident. The Town Hall looks proud and relatively new, and would be well used in this period. The Post Office / General Store is of interest showing the building and the roof structure which was to change considerably over the following years. Note the gable end was to change and the building itself would be somewhat extended. This extension took place in c1904. The village pond is visible near the two standing figures, later to be the site of the War Memorial.

Cross Foxes Public House & Post Office c1920

A popular and interesting image of the village centre taken c1920, with the Cross Foxes Inn very prominent on the left, pictured with the old signage and emblem. The Post Office & General Stores stands proudly in the centre, much changed from the image on page 16. Tai Cochion is just visible on the right, later to become the residence of the village police constable. The cottages on the Cross Foxes yard were demolished in the 1960s at the same time as the Public House was extended.

Pen y felin Road c1960

This c1960 image with presumably Wal Goch farming implements in full view, again just prior to the building of the modern housing development in c1960. The Cross Keys Public House is visible (back left) with the old Post Office (centre) and Tai Cochion cottages very prominent (centre), with the Police Station / House of the time on the right, now reverted back to a private dwelling by the charming name of Bendegedig (Goodbye for now !)

General view, Nannerch c1900

One of the earliest views of the village - difficult to date exactly, but the old Post Office (centre) gives us a definite clue.   This building, now a modern residence, was extended in 1904 (note the gable frontage), thus dating this image to c1900.   This was the general store and Post Office for decades, run by the Fox family, first by the parents and later by their daughter.   The business sadly closed c1959 after a tragic fire incident and was transferred to Nannerch Mill.

Pen y felin Road c1960

This rare photograph of Pen y felin Road taken c1960 before the construction of the modern housing complex. This is the last of three images which are all featured in this publication taken on the same day by Mr R F Higgen, a former resident and keen photographer who lived for many years at Fron Haul.

This image taken from the Cross Foxes car park illustrates how rural and peaceful Nannerch Village was, even in the mid 20th century. The old bench has long since gone and judging by this image the pub car park looked in dire need of resurfacing.

Pen y felin Road today

A present day view showing Pen y felin Road with a better road surface and the introduction of road markings.   Looks like the same telegraph pole has survived and it is certainly in the same place.   Two interesting images depicting how much Pen y felin Road has changed over the last sixty years or so. Hard to visualise that a massive WW1 tank stood on this very corner for nearly two decades.

The Old School, Nannerch.

The old school is situated on what was always known as the Smithy yard. This was the site of the first village school before the present day more modern building was constructed in 1894. The building itself was built in 1836, enlarged in 1845 and improved in 1880. It is now a modern residence, but it is difficult to visualise how all the pupils could fit into the premises, when according to an early school log book, the average attendance in1893 was between 54 and 58 pupils. The Headmaster's house adjoined the old school on the right, with a working Smithy of the time on the left.

School pupils c1890s

This c1890s image of the school children was taken in front of the old school building (see opposite page). Note the same brickwork around the doorway where 28 pupils are featured here, but records suggest that the school complement was much larger. This was taken in the days when education was not entirely free. I believe that a charge was made every Monday morning for the week's tutoring and, in Nannerch's case, reputedly it was three old pence, which is less than one and a half new pence today for a weeks education. A tale related to me years ago, concerning a five year old pupil from the Fron Farm Hendre, turning up on a Monday morning penniless, and was immediately sent home for the fee (a round trip of over four miles) before he could attend class.

Nannerch School

The present school built in 1894, consisted of one large room, which could be partitioned off for the infant sector, the remaining two classes of older children sharing the larger portion.   The building was enlarged gradually over the next century, but the major extension was only built in 1998.   The school was built and greatly supported by the Buddicom family of Penbedw Hall, who maintained this support well into the twentieth century.   The whole building until later years was only heated by two open fires, one in each of the class rooms, and I still recall pupils jostling for benches / desks to be seated near the warm fires.   One former member of staff recalls the school lack off staff cloakroom / toilets, with staff and pupils sharing the same outdoor facilities.   One remarkable fact of the school regarding the headships, is that the school only had two Headmistresses in over half a century (1922-1979) namely, Miss Alwen James and Miss Mair Williams (Roberts) both fondly remembered by older pupils with great affection and regard.

Nannerch School c1955

This c1955 image of the infant class features a dozen local children, many of whom still have strong family connections with the village.

Back row: Roger Morris (Henfaes) / John Verrier / Miss Alwen James (Headmistress)

2nd row: Robert Thomas (Pentref) / David Evans (Bryn Golau) / ? / Ron Williams (Rhyd y Crogwydd) / Alan Watkin (Star Farm)

Front row: Jennifer Kendrick (Lixwm) / Joan Cartwright (Rectory Cottage) / Maureen Jones (Penbedw Mold Lodge) / Connie Jones (Maes yr Esgob) / Rose Roberts (Waen Chapel House)

Nannerch School Pupils 1938

Nannerch School Pupils 1938

A nostalgic image of Nannerch school pupils taken on the last day of term July 1938. Of particular interest to the compiler is that his mother herself is featured in the centre with white shirt and tie on the occasion of her last day at school. An interesting photograph with the absence of any teaching staff. Unable to name all of the pupils but many are remembered fondly by older village families and again many still have strong family connections within the neighbourhood. This image of approximately sixty pupils would in all probability be the entire school complement, with an age group ranging from 5-15. In 1938 one could progress to the grammar school at Mold at the age of 11 years, if successful in passing the 11 plus scholarship or stay at the school until the age of 14 or 15 as was the case of my mother.

Back row boys: ? / Aneurin Hughes / ? / Isaac Roberts / Iori Hughes / ? Jones / ? Byrne / Ralph Byrne / ? / Eddie Cave

Back row girls: Norma Lloyd / ? / ? / Morfydd Jones / ? / Connie Byrne / ? / ? / ? / Peggy Byrne

Second row girls: Dilys Parry / Buddig Williams / ? / Ethel Watkin / Dorothy Pritchard / ? / ? / Muriel Pritchard / Mary Robinson / ? /

First row girls: **Olwen Ellis** / Glenys Jones / Nellie Morris / Doreen Thomas / Joan Evans / Cerys James / ? / Freda James / Renee Jones / Brenda Byrne / June Cartwright

Kneeling: Clifford Halsall / Robert Parry / Glyn Davies / Hwyel Williams / Charles Parry / Llewellyn Jones / Kenneth Williams / Norman Jones / John Morris

Front row: Desmond Hughes / David Jones / Brian Byrne / John Robinson / David Williams / Goronwy Jones / ? / Alfred Jones

Cross Foxes Public House

No publication of the village could possibly be produced without a reference to the old village Inn, probably the oldest surviving building in the village centre and reputedly a licensed premises since c1780. The Inn together with the Church would always have been the hub of the community social life for centuries. The Cross Foxes was reputably built in the 18th century by the Watkin Williams family, who owned Penbedw Estate at the time, hence the title which takes its name from the Family coat of arms. A hostelry in the village for centuries having had to change its image over the period of time. Thankfully it is still a thriving business today which includes a popular catering facility. A meeting place for generations of Parishioners in times gone by, as is the case today. It was particularly well known years ago for the 'sing songs' which were regularly held and enjoyed most weekends. Happy days !

Nannerch Homesteads & Families

The whole area of Nannerch and district is abundant with myths and legends, and to catalogue them all it would take a far larger book than this publication would allow, but many ancient homesteads are situated within its boundaries. For instance, Pen y Garnedd, Penbed Ucha and Nant y Cwm, to name just three examples - all with a tale to tell, and well worthy of more extensive coverage. But, over the centuries, village families have contributed greatly to the well being of the village and its residents and it would be very unfair and unjust to name names, but surely the Buddicom family of Penbedw Hall richly deserve a mention. Over the past generations they had been great benefactors to the Community which, amongst other things, contributed greatly to the School, the Hall and upkeep of the Church, etc., together with the building and maintenance of many farming establishments, as well as providing employment to many village folk.

BUDDICOM FAMILY

PENBEDW HALL

29

Penbedw Hall

Two splendid early 20th century views of the magnificent mansion which graced Penbedw Park for centuries, being situated less than a mile from the village centre. Visible from the main road, the featured building was built in 1770 but greatly improved and enlarged over the years, the last major refurbishment taking place in c1910. This magnificent Hall was at the centre of an estate that boasted over 4,000 acres in it's hay day. The Hall had several large entertaining rooms, with other rooms which included a billiard room and library. It also boasted thirty bedrooms and facilities upstairs, making it a truly palatial structure.

Penbedw Hall

As the image implies, the Hall also enjoyed magnificent gardens, with a full time group of gardeners to oversee its upkeep.   The estate also employed many other different tradesmen and estate workers, ie. Joiners, Blacksmith, Gamekeepers, Laundry staff, Chauffeurs, etc., to name a few occupations which would be needed.   Many of them living in accommodation with their families on the estate itself.   Sadly the Hall itself was demolished in 1958 and the final member of the Buddicom family Venetia died in 1969. The Buddicom family as previously stated were highly thought of and a well respected family in the village and surrounding area for generations.

Town Hall

This small old structure has stood in the centre of Nannerch Village since Victorian times and was once used to house a water pump for the general use of the Community.   A large cast iron working stand pump / pipe was in evidence until the 1950s. This, together with a stone drinking trough for the benefit of passing horses which could be filled from this facility.   It is almost certain that it would be built by the Buddicom family of Penbedw for the use of the village community. The pump itself would be gravity fed from a large steel tank which was and, indeed, still exists above the village close to where the play area is located today.   This brick / stone structure has been a shelter and playhouse for generations of children and was always known locally and affectionately as the Town Hall and is today a Grade II listed building .

Nannerch Memorial Hall

Before 1936 all social activities would have been held in either the Church, School or Public House, but ever since its construction, the building has been the venue for the majority of the village community functions.   Dances and Whist drives, for example, were two of the most popular activities the Hall hosted together with Jumble Sales, Church socials, WI's and more recently Nannerch Players, together with numerous other groups and organisations that have benefited from its existence.   The Hall was enlarged and refurbished in the late 1980s, with the addition of a new Committee Room, Toilets and a Doctors Surgery.   One wartime incident worthy of a mention involved a Mustang fighter aircraft that got into difficulties and crash landed in the adjoining field, sadly killing the pilot, and just missing the building by a matter of inches.

Wedding Party c1937

This image depicts a wedding scene taken outside the Memorial Hall in c1937. It was taken on the occasion of the marriage of Miss Enid Davies to the Revd. Oliver Hill from Llandough (South Wales). Enid was the daughter of Mr & Mrs John Davies from Nannerch Mill who are pictured on the image, together with many close family members, friends and neighbours. Many of those pictured have descendants still living in or with close connections to the village today. The bride is also featured as a small girl on the tank image (page 14) taken nearly twenty years earlier.

Nannerch Memorial Hall

Nannerch Memorial Hall constructed and opened in 1936.   It was a gift to the village from the Buddicom Family of Penbedw Hall as the Memorial plaque states.   In 1935 Venetia Buddicom, together with her mother decided to build a memorial hall for the village in memory of Venetia's father Harry William Buddicom, and her brother Walter Digby Buddicom who was sadly killed in action in WW1 at the young age of 24 after being awarded the Military Cross for outstanding service.   At the time of it's opening it was the envy of all the surrounding villages and the building was also the venue for meeting and training of the local Home Guard during the war time period.   The magnificent oak panelling which adorned the billiard room of the old Penbedw Hall was transferred after the buildings demolition in 1958 and used to line the walls of the Memorial Hall stage.

St Michael & All Angels Parish Church

A modern view of the Church with many of the older sarcophagi and head stones evident.   This being the older section of the churchyard with the later part, which is situated at the top easterly end of the image. The Buddicom vault is situated just behind the trees near left.   This being at least the third church on this site, the first was described as of wattle and daub construction.

St Mary's Church, Nannerch.

This, to the best of my knowledge, is the only image we have of the previous Church which was dedicated to St Mary. Taken from a water colour painting by either Moses Griffiths or John Lloyd which featured in Thomas Pennant's "A tour of Wales" published in 1781. The scene depicts how the building looked in the c1770s. This being the second of three recorded Churches on this site. St Mary's is in the form of a parallelogram with a south facing porch and a wooden steeple at the west, and external steps on the south side leading to a gallery. There doesn't appear to be a Chancel as is the case in the later Church. An interesting view with Llys y Coed and a towerless Moel Fammau noticeable in the background.

St Michael & All Angels Parish Church c1910

The present Church was built in 1852-53 at a cost of £1314.00. It is believed to be at least the third Church on this site, with the first recorded to be made of wattle and daub. A list of former Clergy dates the Church back to at least 1254 and church records from 1664. Always an independent Parish Church until 1968 when it joined with Cilcain and Rhydymwyn Parish Churches sharing a rector.

It is now part of the Bro Fammau Group of Churches. Amongst the memorial / grave stones in the churchyard is the Buddicom family vault - the great benefactors of the village for many years. The image is taken from a picture post card dated 1908. The iron railings have long gone but the yew trees still survive, in all probability older than the Church itself.

Parish Church, Nannerch

Nannerch Church Interior

This c1957 image of Church interior taken on the occasion of the annual Harvest Festival service, always held in early October. Note the abundance of wheat sheaves, flowers, fruit and vegetables, etc. It was a major occasion in the Church calendar when local residents and Parishioners united, and contributed all the produce, filling the building with an abundance of colour and fragrance. This service always preceded the annual Harvest supper, which since 1936 has always been held in the Memorial Hall. Such was the importance of the occasion years ago that the village school children were actually given the full day off school for the preparation and service of the Thanksgiving event.

Pen y felin (Nannerch Mill)

Pen y felin is a small hamlet situated about 3/4 mile to the north of Nannerch. There is a long history of a Mill being in Pen y felin and the Mill is probably the one Edward I granted to the Diocese of St Asaph in 1281. Also, a Mill is mentioned in Edward Lhwyd's Parochial inquiries of 1699. The present Mill was a water powered corn mill first known as Felin Mill and later Nannerch Mill and the present building dates from around 1738 - this information found in the Bishop's Transcripts of Diocese of St Asaph rentals and Nannerch Mill Deeds. Nannerch Mill is one of three mills which operated in the parish, the other two being the Sarn Mill and the Wern Mill. Nannerch Mill was bought and run by the Davies family from around 1885 to 1968. John and Mary Davies and their son John came from Felin Isa, Llandyrnog around 1885. Their daughter Mary was born at Nannerch Mill in 1887. Previously, John and Mary had spent six years in Chicago from 1871-1877.

In the 1901 Census John Davies and his son John were Millers and Bakers employing two servants. They also had expanded into Farming and Mary Davies catered at local events such as the weekly Social evenings and Dances held at Nannerch School.

In 1907 John Davies Jnr married the village blacksmiths daughter Mary Cartwright - they extended the Mill Cottage to include a shop with a bedroom above. Bread, groceries and other household items were sold in the shop, as well as delivering and selling wares around the district using horse and cart.

In 1913 John Davies Jnr took over the family business after the death of his father. He expanded the business further, his foresight being one of first in the area to use commercial motor vehicles which enabled the business to deliver their bread further afield and also cater under huge marquees at all big shows around North Wales, such as Rhyl, Ruthin, Flint and Denbigh, etc. Mr & Mrs Davies, together with their nine children were a well known and respected village family, still remembered fondly by many present day villagers.

During the 1950s and 1960s Nannerch Mill were running four vans for delivering their bread and groceries across North East Wales, as well as catering at all large shows transporting the marquees and equipment by lorry. Around the 1960 they also opened a Post Office counter within the shop. In 1963 John Davies Jnr passed away and his wife Mary Davies (nee Cartwright) having passed away in 1959. Their sons Idwal and Hugh Davies took control of the business until it was sold in 1968.

John Davies & Son (Bakers)

This early c1910 image of Mr John Davies together with members of his family, proudly displaying his horse drawn delivery vehicle. His name together with the home made bread and millers and bakers logo clearly visible. In all probability these two images where taken on the same day. The big roadside stone is evident on both views and the young child is actually sitting on it (page 42). The cart can be seen in front of the Granary.

Nannerch Mill c1910

The first of two picture post card views, taken over a circa fifty year time span in the first half of the last century. A point of interest that both images display the title of Nannerch Mill, but this small hamlet is officially known as Pen y felin, the former was always used colloquially by villagers, certainly when the bakehouse was operational. This early image would be taken not long after the river was bridged, which according to local tradition was sometime in the 1890s. The two figures featured are from all probabilities Mr John Davies of the Mill with one of his family members.

THE NANNERCH MILL

Nannerch Mill c1960

This picture post card was purchased from the Post Office / Shop seen at the near end of the Mill house. It was posted by the compiler to his parents whilst enjoying a two week working holiday at the time helping to deliver bread for the Mill. This c1960 image of the working bakery would be taken approximately a decade before the business folded in 1968. Note the covered canopy by the bakehouse not in evidence on the previous image, but this shelter allowed the delivery vehicles to be loaded out of the elements.

Pen y felin, Nannerch c1937

An interesting old picture postcard view of Pen y felin taken c1937, with Pen y felin Chapel very prominent on the right. This building dating from the 1820s period was a predominantly Welsh speaking Chapel of the Calvinistic Methodist faith, with a membership in excess of 140 once recorded. It served the spiritual needs of the area for approximately 140 years until its closure in c1965 before being converted into a modern residence. The Chapel itself was on the upper storey at road level with the residential premises below.

Pen y felin, Nannerch

A more recent scene of Pen y felin taken in c2000.   Approximately sixty years between the two images.   Tros yr Afon (bottom left) has been significantly modernised as is now the case of Tan y Bryn (bottom centre). The family home of my dear Aunt & Uncle (Edith & Joe Wood) - two well known village characters for over fifty years.   Tros yr Afon (top centre) now firmly established on the hillside would be a newly built property on the previous image. Built by Mr John Davies of Nannerch Mill for one his family members.

The Mill, Nannerch c1910

Two interesting images of an iconic building and business premises that flourished for generations in and around the Parish. Today the old shop, bakehouse and living quarters have been converted into a modern desirable residence of some character. The Granary and store houses on the left have also been converted to modern dwellings. At the nearside of the Granary on the facing gable end would be a water wheel, hidden by the bushes. This implement would be how the corn, etc., was ground and the sole reason why a Mill existed here in the first place. This old wooden / steel structure was working up until the 1960s, but sadly got removed and presumably destroyed at the time of the modernisation of the buildings.

The Mill, Nannerch

It is difficult today viewing the modern image that this small sleepy hamlet was once the centre of a thriving business comprising of a Bakery, major Event Caterers with a Shop, and later Post Office for generations.   In the latter years of trading Nannerch Mill were running four delivery vans across the surrounding countryside, as well as catering at all the large Agricultural and Horticultural shows over a wide area.   Indeed the quality of their bread in particular is still the subject of much favourable debate today by many older residents and customers decades after the business closed. The Fron is very prominent on both images, enlarged and modernised over the century or so between these two views.

Nannerch postcard c1930

A multi-view picture postcard of the village and its surrounds taken c1930.   This is one of a number of picture postcards of the village that has survived the millennia.   Not too many were ever produced, as Nannerch, never being a great holiday destination the demand for such cards was not great.   The surviving postcards are now relatively rare and are of some value.

The Cwm, Nannerch

The Cwm (Pen y felin), Nannerch.

A very rare and interesting picture postcard view of Pen y felin, Nannerch.   The image states The Cwm, but that title was always given to the valley to the right of this image.   Hard to date, but one clue is evident, the Nannerch Mill shop extension which was built in 1907 is just visible seen below the Chapel.   What a wonderful view showing just how rural and sparsely populated this hamlet was in the early part of the last century.

Wheeler crossroads c1910

Always known as the Wheeler crossroads, but how things have changed over the last century or so time difference. The river bridge is not as conspicuous today and the road surface and markings have changed significantly. The bridge itself crosses the upper reaches of the River Wheeler, from where the crossroads, hill and indeed the valley itself gets its very name.

Wheeler crossroads 2017

A familiar modern view of the Wheeler crossroads today, with not so many pedestrians and cyclists in evidence.   I believe many years ago it was a meeting point for locals after Church or Chapel on a Sunday evening from the Lixwm and Nannerch villages to meet regularly - not to fight, but to out sing each other ! How things have changed.   Incidentally, it is on record that the Nannerch lads usually won !

The Wheeler Hill c1920

Looking north from the village in the direction of Lixwm with Tyn y Caeu farmhouse clearly visible on this image.   The Wheeler Cottage (right) has bee n modernised and enlarged over the years.   The home of Mr Isaac Roberts and Family for many years.   Ironically, Mr Roberts was more popularly known as "Ike the Wheeler".   This was a tradition, like in many other villages of the day, where the cottage / farm followed the christian name or, in some cases, surname of the resident.   This was a particular tryst in Nannerch and is still used in many cases nowadays.

The Wheeler Hill 2017

Not too much change over the past century or so, but note the profusion of the woodland in the background which seems to be the biggest difference and, again, the road surface. One noticeable difference between the two images is the lack of walkers on the modern image ! This being a national issue not just appertaining to Nannerch, when years ago before the modern motor car be came popular, walking and horse and cart would be the main mode , if not the only mode of transport in bygone days.

DAVID LLOYD GEORGE GATES

A wonderful pictorial image of rural Nannerch taken in c1908 of Mr Edward Cartwright the village blacksmith. Standing by a set of gates he had been commissioned to make for the great Welsh politician David Lloyd George, seen with the gates in School Lane, with the Smithy buildings on the left and Tyn Llan to the right. Lloyd George would have been Chancellor of the Exchequer at the time before becoming Prime Minister in later years.

Edward Cartwright 1856 /1919 came from a large well known respected family of Blacksmiths of the period. He has been recorded as entering many local and national shows, and Eisteddfod's and was very successful in winning prizes and medals etc at many of these shows. However, his most notable success was at the 1906 London Show, when he was awarded two first prizes for wrought iron gates and a steel door knocker. So impressed was the future Prime Minister, presumably a visitor at the show, with the excellence of his workmanship that he purchased the door knocker and commissioned Mr Cartwright to make a pair of gates for his newly built house at Criccieth. These were duly made and delivered, and he was given a signed certificate and letter of thanks from the honourable gentleman in recognition of his work.

Not only did Mr Cartwright excel with his workmanship on the gates, but he was also a reputed plough maker.   At least one of which went on to win the British Isles Ploughing Championship on several occasions under the very capable control of another villager namely, Mr Tecwyn Morris from the Henfaes.   This very plough now stands as an ornament at Bodvel Hall near Pwllheli with the "Ed Cartwright - Smith - Nannerch" inscription still fully visible dated 1906.

Mr Edward Cartwright c1908

Great Grandson Richard Cartwright

At present these very same gates (page 55) are still in existence at the former Prime Ministers residence of Bryn Awelon, which is now a Nursing Home near Criccieth, with Mr Edward Cartwright's great grandson Richard Cartwright featured.

Flaking a bit of paint here and there, the gates are in as good as condition today as when they were made in c1908. A wonderful testament to the skill and workmanship of the former village Blacksmith.

The old Smithy

Hard to visualise today, but this modern house up until the late 1950s was a working Smithy serving the village and neighbourhood agricultural needs for generations until Mr Jim Williams the last blacksmith in the village retired from the trade to take up general farming at Rhyd y Crogwydd in 1955. The house and smithy was subsequently merged and turned into a modern residential dwelling. Wonderful memories of Mr Williams shoeing horses which we used to witness on our way to and from school.

Nannerch Station c1910

Today it is hard to visualise as one travels along the main Denbigh to Mold highway that for nearly a century a Railway Station and buildings once existed that served Nannerch and its surrounding villages for generations.   Note the smartly dressed presumably local children posing for the camera.   The old road bridge survives to this day, little signs today that this structure carried transport ranging from horse and carts to the modern day auto for almost a century on what was then one of North Wales busiest highways.   A truly nostalgic image of a building and establishment that played such a big part in many past villagers lives.

Nannerch Railway Station

The location of the Railway Station on the Chester to Denbigh line to serve Nannerch and surrounding villages caused great discussion and indeed controversy in the mid 19th century as to the siting of the station.   The villages to the south and easterly (Cilcain / Halkyn Mountain area) argued that the station should be at Maes y Cyffion lands at Star Crossing whilst the northern villages maintained that Nannerch was more favourable and central.

After much debate Nannerch was the selected venue, opening on 6th September 1869.   Star Crossing halt would not be opened until 45 years later in November 1914 adjacent to Maes y Cyffion.   The railway brought many benefits to the village and surrounding areas, ie. coal, milk, livestock, newspapers and mail could all be transported more easily, and later transporting children to the Mold secondary schools.   Also, workers were transported to industries in the wider area, eg. Mold, Chester, Denbigh and De Havilland's Broughton to name just four destinations.   The railway was responsible for new visitors to the district when many local shops and businesses benefited from the influx of tourists, etc., and a new language was heard in the village for the first time (scouse).   The railway was always operated by the LNWR Company from its introduction in 1869 until privatisation in 1923 when it became part of the LMS railway.   This period would be the busiest age of the line.   It was recorded that by 1934 passenger traffic had increased to 13 trains a day in both directions, plus freight trains.

Sadly, after World War 2 with increasing use of private motor vehicles for passengers and freight numbers started to decline and by 1960 only 9 trains with two carriages ran daily from Monday to Saturday.   The line was recommended for closure in 1961, but due to local opposition the announcement was delayed for one year.   The line and station finally closed on the 28th April 1962, when the last trains were packed to capacity both directions with much flag waving and cheering from passengers and locals along the route.   Shortly after closure Nannerch Station was converted into a private residence (see page 62) but soon after this conversion had been completed a compulsory purchase order was made by the local Highway Authorities, together with a row of nearby houses known as Tai Terfyn - all were duly demolished enabling the (A541) highway to follow its original alignment of the old turnpike road over a century previously.

Nannerch Station & Station House c1960

This photographic image was taken just prior to the closure of the station and line in 1962, showing the rear view of the buildings with the ticket office and the waiting room prominent. It is interesting to note that in its prime even a small rural station like Nannerch would employ three or four employees. Many village school children made their way to and from the Mold secondary schools from these premises. The only surviving feature today to give us a clue to the position of the station and buildings is the row of trees on the left of this photographic image.

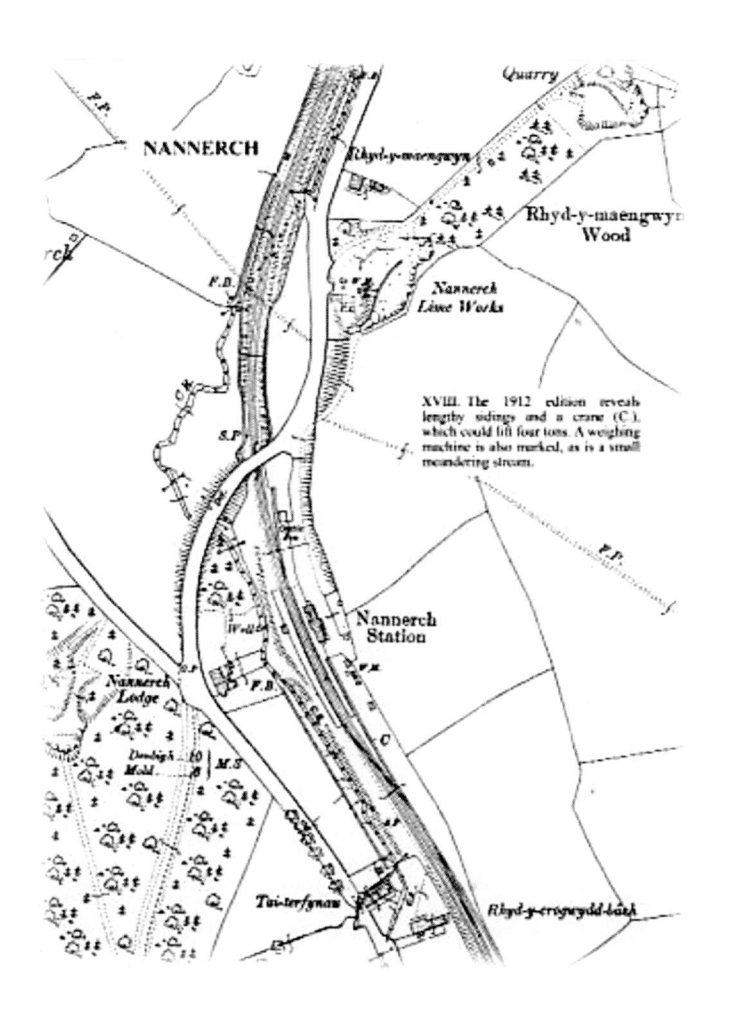

Nannerch Station 1912

This 1912 map shows the station and its surrounds with several points of interest evident. Nannerch Lodge is shown but was often referred to as Station Lodge. Rhyd y Crogwydd Bach (bottom right) was an early coaching station. Rhyd y Maengwyn (ford of the white rock) with Nannerch lime works in close proximity. The position of Tai Terfynau now sadly demolished is evident (bottom centre). A public footpath is shown which was the route the compiler often trod to and from school on a daily basis.

Old Station Buildings c1970

A rather sad and poignant photographic image of the old railway station buildings after its major renovation / refurbishment. This image was taken c1970 just prior to its demolition, to enable the A541 trunk road to follow its original route. The house was fully modernised, but a compulsory order was granted and the property was duly demolished, together with the destruction of the newly laid out gardens which were situated between the two platforms.

Nannerch Station c1960

This tranquil image of the old station and house taken from a picture post card posted in the 1930s. This image would be taken looking in the direction of Mold from near the old road bridge which is still evident today. An old railway hut is the only surviving structure (2018) from a truly bygone age. It is impossible today to gauge the impact that the railway had on small rural communities such as Nannerch. Just getting to Mold for example by horse and float must have been an arduous task taking over an hour at best, but the new mode of transport could do the journey in a matter of minutes. The route the line took between Nannerch and Star Crossing is of interest, because the planners of the 1860's wanted to run the line nearer or indeed through Penbedw Park. Mr Buddicom strongly opposed the Bill and was able to realign the route through a man made cutting to enable it to be screened from the Hall.

Star Crossing Halt

An interesting image of Star Crossing Halt just prior to its closure. Looking in the direction of Nannerch, it was opened in 1914 to satisfy the transportation needs of the nearby villages of chiefly Cilcain and the Halkyn Mountain villages. It was also the highest point in altitude on the Chester to Denbigh branch line. The railway crossing gates were hand operated by the Gateman / Porter employee, from early morning until late at night residing in the railway cottage.

The hills, Nannerch.

This c1930s old picture postcard view taken from the Star Crossing looking west, with the Clwydian mountain range in the background and, in particular, Moel Plas Yw prominent on the left, with the definitive Moel Evan in the centre. The main drive to Penbedw hall is very evident through the trees, obviously much used during this period. Tyn Twll can be seen behind the big tree in the centre.

The Bryn Hill, Nannerch.

Bryn Hill, Nannerch

A familiar view of the main thoroughfare into and out of the village from the south. Seldom called Bryn Hill nowadays, but presumably named from the nearby residence which is named The Bryn (Welsh for hill). This residence was the home of the Laird family of Camel Lairds the famous ship builders for many years. The corner on the right side was improved in a road widening scheme several years ago.

GENERAL VIEW, NANNERCH.

General View, Nannerch.

This unusual view of the area, taken from a c1920 picture postcard, illustrates a general view of Nannerch, looking north easterly in the direction of Lixwm, with Pyw Gwyn Farm on the right, Coed y Brain top left and Garneddwen top centre all very prominent. The main road, railway and Wheeler river would all follow the valley just beyond the second hedgerow. This image is taken from the top of the Wheeler hill near to where Penrallt is situated. This view today is difficult to replicate because of the increased forestation and greenery that exists today.

The hanging tree !

Allegedly this former hangman's tree can still be seen in the field opposite where Rhyd y Crogwydd Bach is situated today. In ages past there would have been a ford nearby where the upper reaches of the Afon Chwiler crossed the old coach road, hence the word Rhyd.   An old c1970s magazine article by Hazel Formby may throw some light on the subject.   She states that years ago it was well established practice that thieves convicted of highway robberies would be strung up at or near to the scene of the crime.   If a malefactor had given his life here, a record would have been made of the event, but just as easy it could have been lost !   How else but by the presence of a gallows tree could the very name of Rhyd y Crogwydd possibly be derived ?   The above image was taken in c1970 and features the Seaburg family who at the time resided at Rhyd y Crogwydd Bach.

Rhyd y Crogwydd

Not every residence of the Parish can possibly be included in such a small publication, but the legend of this particular homestead and site I believe fully warrants an inclusion. The very title is translated into English as The Hanging or Gallows ford !   Rhyd y Crogwydd was like many other properties in the area, part of the Penbedw Estate.   The present building dates from 1905, having replaced an earlier structure on or near to the same site.

PENBEDW DRIVE, NANNERCH   "The Unique Series"

Penbedw Drive

An old picture postcard view of Penbedw Drive, but always locally known as the village / station drive. This is one of three routes that exists from the main road up to the Hall & Estate.   This particular drive exits near the Nannerch / Station Lodge.   Village folk used to relate the tale that the drive was swept weekly prior to the family making their way from the Hall to the village Church every Sunday. The main drive to the Hall was from Mold Lodge.   This drive is little used today, but still can still be followed, and is lined by an avenue of old copper Beech trees, which were planted as a memorial to W B Buddicom who was sadly killed in WW1.

Penbedw Lodge

Although called Penbedw Lodge on the postcard, this building was always known as either Station Lodge or Nannerch Lodge. Dated 1875 this semi-detached building was one of three such lodges to grace the Estate entrances. The other two being, Middle Lodge and Mold Lodge. The Middle Lodge 400 yards south stood on the corner of the then predominantly tradesmen's entrance whilst Mold Lodge at Star Crossing affectionately guarded the main drive. Cilcain Hall Lodge was a further half mile in the Mold direction. It is of interest that this particular lodge was designed by John Douglas in the same era and style as Tai Cochion.

Plas Yw

One of the oldest premises / sites surviving in the parish today is Plas Yw. Described in one history book as being an ancient residence of some distinction which was once moated, and reputed to be the abode for refuge of Owain Glyndwr at the time of his rebellion in the early 1400s.   Also referred to on the act of union map of 1541 classifying it as a gentry house.   Near the premises can be found the remains of a bronze age earthen built round barrow, a monument of national importance, one of several in the area.   Plas Yw was the home of the compilers family in the mid 1920s albeit for only two years, a building that has hardly changed significantly for centuries.

Wal Goch

This late 1950s image of Wal Goch claiming to be a two storey L shaped medieval farm house dating from the 1530s Tudor era. Indeed the very building structure design depicts a residence from the early to mid 14 century period. The frontage which features a cyclopean doorway, porch with heraldry / crest of a medieval design above. A shield / coat of arms which was popular during the renaissance period when this building would have been constructed. The house itself was reputed to be a Bishop's retreat within the Diocese of Chester and in all probability correct, but unable to verify the fact. The property was known as Nannerch Hall until the mid 19th century, when it changed its name to the less grandeur title of Wal Goch. Interestingly, this property is just one of 27 listed buildings / structures in the Parish of Nannerch remaining today.

ACKNOWLEDGMENTS

During the research and preparation of this book, I have had the pleasure of the company and gained the knowledge of many past and present Nannerch residents, and to name them all would be difficult and unfair, but several individuals I do feel particularly grateful to, and feel an acknowledgment is necessary and fully justified :-

    Clifford Halsall

    Richard Cartwright - Image page 55

    Capt. Nicholas Archdale - Images pages 29, 30

    Owen Thomas

    Hazel Formby - page 68

    Beryl Williams - Images page 62, 68, 69

    E. Douglas Wrench (Church data)

    David Higgen - Images pages 6, 18, 20

    Flintshire Record Office - Images pages 6, 18, 20, 72, 73

    Clwyd-Powys Archaeological Trust - Image page 2

And, last but not least, my good lady wife Sonja, who without her help, typing and computer skills, I personally could not possibly have produced this book.